ISBN 978-0-484-59680-0
PIBN 10057655

istence of heavenly Sovereign, what you adore by day will be your destruction by night."

By not disapproving this act of government, this blasphemy is the blasphemy of the nation, and of all, who unite with them. This same power is in the habit of "great words." They declare, "Death is an eternal sleep." There is the essence of practical blasphemy. The same Power "changes times and laws;" they change the sabbath; instead of a sabbath of holy praise one day in seven; they establish a gay festival one day in ten. They "change laws." Without fleets or seamen, with a single "imperial decree," they blockade the harbors of the commercial world. The students of a public school are introduced to the Legislature. In his address one of the pupils says, "I and my companions *detest a God.*" The nation received this with applause. Does not this Power "speak great words against the Most High?"

St. Paul draws this Power in more vivid and distinct colors. "In the last days perilous times shall come; for men shall be lovers of their own-selves, covetous, boasters, proud, blasphemers, without natural affection, truce-breakers, false accusers, incontinent, fierce, despisers of those who are good, traitors, heady, high minded, having a *form* of godliness, but denying the *power*."* "Boasters" they are. Did ever a nation show such a "proud," boastful, overbearing spirit toward other nations? Their blasphemies need not be mentioned again. They are "without natural affection."† It has been a favorite object of organized societies and volumes have

* 2 Tim. 3.

† See Payson's Modern Anti-Christ.

Levi Lincoln

A SERMON, &c.

REVELATION, 18, 4.

And I heard another voice from heaven saying: Come out of her, my people, that ye be not partakers of her sins, and that ye receive not of her plagues.

AS a kind parent warns his children of approaching danger; so God warns his people to secure themselves from divine judgments. As a faithful centinel descries danger, and alarms the camp; so God calls upon the armies of his people to be prepared for the day of sorrow. Dangers are marked with precision; the path of duty is enlightened with the brightest sun-beams of heaven. The errors and delusions of the world are therefore only proofs, that the heart is perverse, that the fountain of action is corrupted. If men are blind, it is merely because they will not see. If they proceed in a wrong course, it is merely because they are averse from good. The commands and threatnings of God's word proceed on the ground that men have sufficient light and knowledge. In the text therefore God says, " Come out of her, my people, that ye be not partakers of her sins, and that ye receive not of her plagues." A false church, a community of hypocrites, a class of sinners, are supposed to be so malignant, so con-

Ruin or Separation from Anti-Christ.

A Federal Sermon

A

SERMON

PREACHED AT BYFIELD,

APRIL 7, 1808,

ON THE ANNUAL FAST

IN THE

COMMONWEALTH OF MASSACHUSETTS.

" Who gave commission to these monsters *fierce*,
" To hold in chains the humble universe?
" The direful signs, which mark the day of doom,
" Will scarcely scatter such portentous gloom.
" When rock'd the ground, convuls'd each roaring flood,
" The stars shall fall, the sun be turn'd to blood."

BY ELIJAH PARISH, D. D.
MINISTER OF BYFIELD.

NEWBURYPORT....*E. W. & W. B. ALLEN*, PRINTERS.
APRIL—1808.

been written, to prove that man is a cosmopolite, a citizen of the world, that he has no appropriate duties as a subject, a citizen, or the father of a family. They are "Truce-breakers." The ruling power of Europe observes treaties no further than interest, convenience, and ambition, require. At the present moment our country is suffering, our prosperity is sinking, and our ships are blazing in violation of solemn treaties. "False accusers" they are. Of their own best people, millions have been beheaded, and drowned, and butchered by false accusations.* The history of the world does not present a more astonishing example of falshood, of blood, and barbarism. St.Paul declares them "incontinent" or unchaste. Their passing history declares the same, that they have virtually abrogated the ordinance of marriage by the facility of divorces. How literally, how *precisely* they answer the description of Anti-Chtist you may learn, if I can persuade myself to recite a decree of the nation in 1794. "It is there declared that there is nothing criminal in the promiscuous intercourse of the sexes." Forgive me this freedom. It is of infinite importance that you know the enemy from whom you must separate. We need no additional facts to illustrate the fierceness of this power. "Fierce" she is "as ten furies and terrible as hell." Her fury is consuming the nations of Europe. By St. Paul they are called "Traitors." This single word remarkably distinguishes this power. The reigning power was built on the ruins of the consular government; the consular government was built on the ruins of the republic; the

* See Residence in France. Kett, Clergy's Journal, &c.

republic rose from the ashes of the monarchy. Insurrection and rebellion after rebellion; perjury after perjury, and treason after treason, produced the present stupendous power of the empire. Surely no power was ever more justly branded with the name of "Traitor." The prophet of Tarsus distinguishes this empire by its "having the *form* of godliness, but denying the *power*." The mighty Colossus, which tramples on the powers of the European continent, has established the false religion of Rome, as a political engine, having no more reverence for this religion, than for the delusions of Mahomet, or the superstition of paganism. When in a Mahometan country, he declares himself a believer in Mahomet, and boasts that he has destroyed the religion of Christ in Europe. Since the world begun there never has been a more remarkable, more notorious instance of a people, having the form of godliness and denying the power.

By this time no reflecting mind can be at a loss, who those are from whom we are commanded "to come out." Still more witnesses press to be heard. From the cavern of Patmos, St. John* declares, this "Beast causeth all, both small and great, rich and poor, bond and free, to receive a mark," or token of their respect for him; in a sovereign manner he considers them on his side, as his servants.† He "decrees" that "no man might buy or sell, save he that had the mark," or token of subjection to him. Observe, he "caused;" a very general word.

* Chap. 13. † See a late communication from our Minister at the Court of France.

He has not fleets to *compel;* but partly by force, partly by imperial decrees, and partly by "diplomatic skill," he "*causes*" the traffic of the nations to suffer. The hum of business is silent; commercial fleets no longer whiten every sea. Individual cities have, before, lost their commerce; the commerce of a nation has been for a short time suspended; the Pope has sometimes controled the commerce of the church; but this is the era in which we hear a voice forbidding "all men," excepting the vassals of the "Beast" "to buy or sell."* As it was with the city of Tyre, so it is now with all our commercial cities. "And all that handle the oar, the mariners and the pilots of the sea, shall come down from their ships; they shall stand upon the land, and shall cause their voice to be heard against thee, and shall cry bitterly; and cast dust upon their heads, and wallow themselves in ashes." Every day and hour make the picture plainer and plainer. Do not the friends of this power daily boast that no King nor Emperor can resist his force, that he can subdue the frozen Russians, and triumph in the spicy groves of India. So Revelation says, "Power was given the beast over all kindreds, and tongues, and nations." Where his arms cannot reach, the influence of his agents prevails from the Baltic to the Archipelago, from Constantinople to Washington.

II. What is implied in "coming out" from this tremendous power.

* Our veſſels are now detained in France, that they may aſcertain whether we will unite with her, and receive the mark of the beaſt. Then it is intimated we may "buy and ſell." See communications from our miniſter in France.

1. We must come out from them in heart and spirit. The words of the address are worthy of notice. "Come out, my people ;" my people of every country, nation and language ; in every city, village, and family of the world. As this Anti-Christian power first rose out of the church, and is in itself an apostate church, her poison may be expected wherever God has a people ; wherever there is a wreck, or remnant, or name of a church ; because where true believers are, where the wheat is, there is the chaff and the tares. This Hydra walks in darkness, and like pestilence and death is every where. We may, possibly, find the serpents in our most sacred connexions, in the church, in our families. The husband of a pious wife ; the child of a pious parent, may be a limb of the "beast." "Come out from them, my people, in all the vast dominions of this mighty usurpation, saith the Lord, as far as may be consistent with other positive and sacred obligations. Families need not separate, nor subjects leave their country nor government ; yet they may in heart and spirit come out from them ; they may abhor their principles, detest their designs, and as far as possible, counteract their fatal measures.

2. We must separate from them by incessantly praying against their malignant influence. A large portion of the civilized world is divided into two great sections. Whatever may be the character of each individual in either section, the general tendency of one is to support, of the other to destroy the cause of Jesus Christ. It is our duty to pray that these may be disappointed in their designs against the cause of the Re-

deemer; it is our duty to pray like the Psalmist, "Grant not the desire of these wicked men." Prayer is a duty, tho' the friends of Anti-Christ point the finger of scorn. In answer to prayer, seas have divided their billows, rivers stopped in their course; the sun and moon stood still; how much more will God hear us, when we pray against bold blasphemers.

3. Of course, in no instance can we "bid them God speed," or rejoice in their success.

If in the most secret manner we rejoice at their success; if we breathe a congratulation in our hearts; we then approve their character; we partake in their sins; we must receive their plagues. To rejoice in iniquity is ourselves to be guilty.

4. To come out from this power, we must resist his influence by all lawful means.

Here opens a wide field, which cannot be thoroughly explored. Personal circumstances, the state of society, the events of the moment, must direct every man to his post, and the part he is to perform. Arguments, exhortations, petitions, and entreaties; a most firm use of our privilege of suffrage; all may be powerful means to repel the force, and bridle the ferocity of the beast with whom we contend. For parents to instruct their children in sound principles; for the rich to encourage the poor, who are honest, in preference of those who are the base slaves of slaves; for ministers to instruct their people concerning the real state of the church and the world, may powerfully resist this gangrene of moral death. The most wanton government is to be resisted only in a lawful manner. Nero and Napoleon, kings and presidents, while on the throne, must be obeyed. We must obey them *for the Lord's sake.* We honor their office, tho' we recoil from their characters; we obey their laws, tho' we resist their dangerous influence. And I heard another voice from heaven, saying, "Come out from among them, my people, that ye partake not in her sins, and receive not her plagues."

III. What plagues or judgments will those endure, who do not separate from this Anti-Christian power?

1. They shall imbibe her spirit, assume her character. They shall receive *her* plagues; the same, which she endures herself. This is the plague of all plagues. Rather let famine, war and pestilence, arrest us, than the malignant, contagious spirit of Anti-Christ. What this spirit is you have *in part* just heard, and may better learn from a thousand sources daily opening before you.

Infidelity is a prominent feature of the haggard countenance we are examining. The ruling power of Europe has long been determined to pull up religion by the roots, to cast this tree of Paradise into the fire of their vengeance. They have determined to destroy the *means* of its existence. Not a pastor shall be allowed to feed the sheep or the lambs of Christ's flock. In proof of this we inform you from French papers, which for once we believe are correct: That in the time when more than one hundred ministers of religion ~~has~~ have died, only four had been ordained to supply their places. It appears also that in a country where there were five thousand vacancies, not fifty candidates

have

were known to supply them. The salaries allowed are denominated starving jokes, and supposed to be directed by the government to destroy christianity by destroying her ministers. They are compelled to engage in other callings to support themselves. So penurious is their reward ; so abject, so miserable, their situation. The people are so poisoned with infidelity ; they are so hardened by the spirit of Anti-Christ, that they refuse to pay the smallest tax to support a seminary for clerical education. So few are the churches, supplied with pastors, that those who are hungry for the bread of life, and thirsting for the waters of salvation, are obliged to travel forty, fifty and sixty miles to find a place where a minister officiates. Two million Protestants in France are in this deplorable situation, almost twice as many as all the inhabitants of New-England.

But our object is in view. The command is, "Come out of her, my people, that ye receive not of her plagues." One of the plagues of these self-destroyers is to be like this power to whom they adhere. In order to ascertain what this is, we have been so particular. She is rampired round with infidelity, and daring impiety. She despises the ordinances, the churches, the christian ministry. Her language is, " where is the promise of his coming?" "The doctrines of ministers and christians are idle dreams."

Sometimes God gives up the wicked to commit sin with all greediness, as a part of their punishment for other sins ; he withdraws his Holy Spirit, and they believe a lie, that they may be damned. So those, who will not come out from Anti-Christ, are left to become like Anti-Christ.

We drop speculating on the subject, and appeal to facts, to facts of which you are all the best judges. Is it then, or is it not, a solemn fact, as far as mortals can discern, or as far as your acquaintance extends, that those who do not come out from this infidel power, do possess a great degree of her spirit? Observe the most respectable of this description. You are pleased with their address; you respect their talents; you honor their profound science; but you wishfully and anxiously inquire for somewhat that will mark *a character* opposite to Anti-Christ. Again you ask, you inquire, you look; but *do* you ever see them shudder at the enormities and horrors of French infidelity? Do you ever hear them lament the irreligion, the impiety, the barbarism, the oppressions and slaughters of blasphemous Anti-Christ? Do they not make a multitude of excuses and apologies; do they not fill their mouth with arguments to justify her? Do they not *harmonize* with Anti-Christ? Who are they, that are little hurt, and readily connive at the most open contempt of divine things, at ridicule cast on the doctrine of the deluge, the volume of revelation itself, and the gospel ministry? Need we *name* them? Who are they, who in general display in a great degree the spirit of Anti-Christ himself? "Do ye not know them by these tokens?" They have begun to receive the plagues mentioned in the text. Let the devout spirit exclaim, "Oh my soul, come not thou into their secret; mine honor, be not thou joined with them."

2. Another plague of Anti-Christ is to endure the greatest political oppression and servitude.

The people of that devoted country, to which we have constant reference, are broken by the hand of oppression; they are crushed by the iron foot of a tyrant. Even liberty of speech is denied; a large proportion of the inhabitants are spies, in the pay of government, to catch the words of their neighbors, their companions, their friends. No man dares to make remarks on the measures of government, lest a spy should complain, and his life pay for his words. A paper in this state has lately intimated, that it may soon be "political suicide" to animadvert on the conduct of the administration; the expression of opinion has been represented as treason. Tho' we find it difficult to conceive that such arrogance exists; yet it is too probable we may soon feel the sword of such a law in our own vitals. Then those persons, so zealous now to pull these calamities on our heads, will be equal sufferers; then will they execrate their union with anti-christian darkness; then will they not be allowed the privilege of the Egyptians to raise a great cry, when there is one dead in every house.

The contributions levied, the taxes imposed on the "allies" of France, exceed description, and baffle calculation. A late traveller mentions, that in Lombardy the inhabitants pay one half their annual income to the French government. Would the time permit, we might travel all over Europe, and find occasion for similar remarks. Prussia is suffering inexpressible distress; the people are fainting with their burdens, and mad with despair. In Germany, war, disease and famine, have overwhelmed the inhabitants. In the scarcity of bread, they have been compelled to feed on grass.* So deplorable is their situation, that great sums have been raised in England for their relief. Genoa, saith the Marquis Salvo, is stripped of its property, driven to the last state of wretchedness, her commerce completely annihilated. From Hanover and other parts of Germany, the inhabitants are flying into Austria, and are even there refused the protection of the government. Does not this indicate the lowest state of misery ! Portugal has paid tribute till she could pay no longer. When her circulating medium was exhausted, she plundered her own churches of their plate and ornaments to appease the insatiable tyrant.† Nor would this suffice ; his armies now occupy the country, live upon the inhabitants ; famine and misery follow. The king and royal family have fled to America. Switzerland is compared to the skin of a beast, offered in sacrifice. She has been robbed, and plundered, and ruined, by the terrible republic. Like the skin of a victim deprived of its body and its life, its bones and marrow, they are trodden under the feet of their masters. Her racks, demagogues and ruins, are all that remain. Those plagues, like an overwhelming deluge, are rushing on all nations, who do not come out from this mighty power.

3. Everlasting destruction is the portion of Anti-Christ, and of all who do not separate from him.

rocks

* See Panoplist, Vol. 1. † Letter from Lisbon.

Rev. 14 chap. And the third angel followed, saying, with a loud voice, "If any man worship the beast and his image, and receive his mark," become his friend or agent, "the same shall drink the wine of the wrath of God, which is poured forth without mixture into the cup of his indignation, and he shall be tormented with fire and brimstone in the presence of the holy angels, and in the presence of the Lamb, and the smoke of their torment ascendeth up forever and ever, and they have no rest day nor night, who worship the beast or his image," or are friendly to this Infidel power, "or receiveth the mark of his name," or becometh subject to his influence.

Chap. 19. After these things I heard another voice of much people in heaven saying, "Alleluia," and again they said, "Alleluia," and her smoke rose up forever and ever, and the four and twenty Elders worshipped God, saying, "Amen; Alleluia."

IMPROVEMENT.

One interesting reflection forces itself upon our attention, it has doubtless been made by every hearer, this Commonwealth and the country must detach themselves from Anti-Christ or be destroyed.

Has not this Commonwealth and the United States, once and again elected those Legislators whom they intended should be friendly, and *partial* to the interests of Anti-Christ? Those, who unite and coalesce with her, will inevitably fall; those, who daringly resist her, will ride out the storm, which now shakes the foundations of the world. If Sweden and Great-Britain make peace, and form an alliance with their foe, that moment, are they like Sampson in the lap of the harlot, exposed to have their locks shorn, their eyes torn out, to lose their liberty and their existence.

That these opinions will be treated with contempt and scorn, it may be expected; the children of Lot ridiculed his story of fire from heaven; doubtless the Anti-deluvians derided Noah for his ship, his navigation, and his tale of a universal deluge. One great infelicity of ridicule and contempt is, they have never been found a secure defence against the judgments of God. With all their sport Sodom was burned; the world was drowned. Had I a voice to be heard from Maine to Georgia, gladly would I meet the torrent of sarcasms, which, like the foam of Niagara, might burst forth, for the privilege of commenting on the text, and most affectionately warning the people. It is, *it is* a day of darkness and rebuke. Never was there a louder call for a day of humiliation and prayer. Never was a greater deliverance to be prayed for, deliverance from the plagues of Anti-Christ.

The sparks, which will inevitably consume us unless we repent are already kindled. The clouds, charged with the thunders of desolation, are spreading their dark shadows over the land. That oppression, that infidelity, that impiety, which are plagues of Anti-Christ, are already visible, and good men tremble. A deplorable evil it is to belong to a community, devoted to ruin; yet God sometimes delivers those, not guilty of procuring the judgments ; but he is under no obligation to do this. The personal sins of the best men would justify Providence in punishing them with his enemies. As a nation we sin, and as a nation we may be destroyed. Yet may we pray for deliverance in the day of wrath. When Jerusalem was sacked by Titus, the christians, being warned by Christ, fled from the city, and escaped the undescribable horrors of the siege. When Rome was taken by Alaric the Goth, Honorius, and other christians, were secure in Ravenna.

Leaving it to every one to make a more formal application for himself, we beg your patience a moment, while we sincerely and tenderly entreat you, not to consider this a party discourse, or an effusion of the moment. No. These hasty hints are well founded ; they are the words of truth and soberness. They are supported by existing *events*, as well as the word of God. A man must be blind to the history of recent events, as well as dead to christian faith to controvert these opinions. The Preacher begs you to consider this as a plain, practical discourse ; the duties, as important as can be recommended. Those, who trifle with these warnings, he views in a situation more alarming than the murderer. The murderer finds no one to justify him ; he hears a thousand reproofs, and is alarmed ; but in your friendship to Anti-Christ, more than half the nation justify the deed of impiety, hand joins in hand, and a covenant with hell is confirmed. But do remember, that whatever else you doubt, or deny, *the text is the word of God ;* the text refers to Anti-Christ ; not to know, who is Anti-Christ, must argue gross ignorance of the bible, and the world. Be so kind, so merciful to yourselves, as to remember, the text implies that, our ruin or salvation depends on our conduct towards this Infidel power, which is covering the world with darkness. Our prosperity and our destruction are before us. The choice is ours. If you believe the word of God ; if you only attend to passing events, it will be easy to decide on this important subject.

Only *look* at the nations of Europe. Which of them have suffered most ; which of them have suffered least by that Power, who makes the earth drunk with blood ? It is a truth recorded in every page of passing events, that those nations have suffered most, who have been most friendly to this Anti-Christian Power, who have lent their assistance, and courted her favor. It is a glorious truth that those have suffered the *least*, who have unfurled the banner of defiance, and waged incessant war with Anti-Christ, and all his mercenary legions.

Spain has been the friend and ally of this gigantic power, supported her measures, and been the instrument of her iniquities, yet now she sees those fortresses, which are the keys of the country, which are of essential importance to the well-being of the State, resigned to the legions of France. The king himself is little better than a cypher or royal captive in his own palace. The United Provinces, Switzerland, Portugal, some States of Germany, have distinguished themselves as the friends of this mighty Foe to

Jesus Christ; they have presented most flattering addresses; they have received his soldiers as brethren, and the valiant friends of *liberty*. What have been the consequences? These countries have been overrun with desolating armies; they have been plundered and murdered; their harvests have vanished from their fields; their sick have been torn from their beds, their houses have been barracks for French soldiers; their sons and husbands have been dragged into the armies of the Conqueror, to bleed and die unpitied and unknown; their daughters and wives have been polluted by the legions of Anti-Christ; their governments are dissolved, and their names are blotted from the catalogue of Nations.

On the other hand, "the mother country," the blest land of our fathers sepulchres, Great-Britain, has nobly dared to wage a just war with this blasphemous Power. What have been the consequences? Her fields have never been robbed or defiled by the troops of Napolean; they have never spread desolation along the fair coast of England; they have never profaned her churches, nor dragged her sons into their bloody armies; the navies of England ride triumphant in every sea; they chastise her enemies; they waft to her ports the comforts and luxuries of every clime. Such is the fruit "of coming out" from Anti-Christ; while we and other nations, like moles and bats, crawl at the feet of the Conqueror; like serpents eat the dust of his feet, or are chained to his car to swell the splendor of his triumphs. Our incalculable sacrifices; our loss of ships, our tribute, our suspension of commerce, are entirely the fruit of our friendship to Anti-Christ. The present state of the world, is a lucid comment on our text. Those, who deny our text, or our construction of it, ought to be ignorant of passing events in Europe and America, to claim any particle of consistency or integrity. Those, who have *not* come out from this Power have partaken in her sins, and are now, *now* actually receiving her plagues. Our country has begun to sip the deadly draught; others have drunk the very dregs. Be warned then, oh my friends, my beloved people. As the warnings of Jonah shook the walls of Nineveh, so should the voice in the text awaken your fears. An enemy is at hand; he is not a trifling enemy. He is a strong man armed, and as *artful*, as he is strong. He deceives whom he cannot subdue. His friends are as bold as guilt and despair can make them. They have no hope, but in the success of this arch enemy of Jesus Christ. Their union seems indissoluble; they are joined by bands of iron. As the Egyptians *unitedly* pursued their revenge of Israel into the abyss of the sea; so these men, although their chariot wheels drag heavily, seem resolved to brave all the dangers and terrors before them. As in a storm, when all hope is lost, sailors seize the flowing bowl, that in drunkenness they may deaden the horror of going down together; so this unhappy fraternity inflame themselves with party spirit, that they may laugh at destruction, and sport with the awful doom, bursting on themselves and their country. As "devil with devil damned firm concord holds"; so these maintain a horrid combination of spirits, and bid defiance to conviction.

Beloved, though we thus speak, we hope better things of you; still it may be wise to examine yourselves; we beseech you to examine your hearts to the bottom; see if there be no seeds of this contagious infidelity; no spark of this unhallowed fire, smothered in any corner of your hearts. Merely joining with that section of the public whose object it is to support religion, will not, cannot save you. Personal virtues you must possess. Though none of you, as far as we know, are so lost to religious impressions, as to act in concert with the friends of Anti-Christ; yet are you never secretly pleased with their dreadful spirit and character? Do you never secretly rejoice to see them carry havoc into the vineyard of Christ, afflict his servants, and trample on the fruits of their labors?

If you value your own peace and safety here; if you would not pull down the judgments of God on your families, your neighbors, and your country; if you would not with all the friends of Anti-Christ sink into that lake, which burneth forever and ever; then fly from this unholy enemy. What communion hath light with darkness; what concord hath Christ with Belial? "And I heard another voice from heaven saying, Come out of her, my people, that ye be not partakers of her sins, and that ye receive not of her plagues." AMEN.

NOTES FOR PAGE 7.

The executions in Paris in one month, July 1794, were 88 ministers, 305 nobles, 530 of the people, total 929. *Playfair.*

A child of ten years of age had been corrected by its mother. He ran to the revolutionary tribunal, and accused her of being still attached to the catholic religion. The accusation was received; the boy rewarded, and the mother executed in a few hours. *History of the French Clergy.*

Goullin beat his own father with a stick, when the old man was on his death bed; the father died in two hours. *ibid.*

The obedience of the child to the father was called a remnant of *feudal slavery.*

NOTES FOR PAGE 12.

Camus and Condorcet, leaders in the national legislature, openly taught atheism; and another of them, Ceruti, said with his last breath, "The only regret, which I have in quitting the world, is that I leave a *religion* on the earth." Such would be "the blasphemy" of expiring demons. *Barruel.*

Sept. 3. Philippé came to the Jacobin club, of which he was a member with a box in his hand; he made an harangue, declaring those worthy of death that preferred the ties of blood to those of patriotism, and to prove his sincerity, opened the box and held up the heads of his father and mother, "*which I have cut off,*" said he, because they refused to hear mass from an apostate priest. Jacobins of late have ycleped themselves republicans. *Hist. of the French Clergy.*

When I was in France I faw fufficient reafon to believe, that hardly any perfon of eminence, was a believer in Chriftianity; and no perfon will fuppofe there has been any change in favor of Chriftianity. *Dr. Prieftly.*

Gobet, the bishop of Paris with his grand vicars, and three revolutionary priefts in the hall of the Legislators, abdicated Chriftianity in form; they begged pardon of the nation for duping them into a belief of the divinity of an Impoftor, and declared they acknowledged no Deity, but Reafon. *Barruel.*

NOTES FOR PAGE 16.

More than £17,779 sterling, have been contributed in England for the fufferers in Germany, beside various sums in Scotland. *Religious Monitor.*

Having been obliged to supply French armies with provision and clothing, cities and villages being crouded, last summer there was fuch a scarcity in several parts of Saxony, Silesia, Bohemia, Auftria, and other provinces, that many baked bran for bread, and used grafs for vegetables. Some people went even to those places where dead horses were thrown, and fed upon their carcases. Such is the misery of French amity. The breath of the monfter is fatal; her contagion is death. *See Panoplift, Vol. I.*

ERRATA.

Page 6, line 10 from top, for promise *read* praise——p. 12, l. 4 from bottom, for has *read* have——p. 13, l. 2 from top, for jokes *read* stipends——p. 16, l. 7 from bottom, for racks *read* rocks.

[Sold at the Book-Store of THOMAS & WHIPPLE.]

CPSIA information can be obtained
at www.ICGtesting.com
Printed in the USA
BVHW04*1357210918
528174BV00011B/608/P

9 780484 596800